UNIVERSITY & COLLEGE

STUDENTS' SUCCESSFUL SURVIVAL HANDBOOK

First Edition

By

Emmanuel M. Chijioke, Ph.D, JD
Dean and Prof. of Business/Law
Stillman College, Tusc., Alabama, 35401

Copyright © 2014 by Emmanuel M. Chijioke, Ph.D., JD

University & College- Students' Successful Survival Handbook
College & University Students' Survival in the 21st Century
by Emmanuel M. Chijioke, Ph.D., JD

Printed in the United States of America

ISBN 9781498419192

All rights reserved solely by the author. The author guarantees all contents are original and do not infringe upon the legal rights of any other person or work. No part of this book may be reproduced in any form without the permission of the author. The views expressed in this book are not necessarily those of the publisher.

Scripture quotations taken from the King James Version (KJV) – public domain

www.xulonpress.com

Presented To:

_____

_____

From:

_____

_____

Date:

_____

_____

Students' Successful Survival Handbook

By

Emmanuel Chijioke

CONTENTS

Preface and Acknowledgment .... *xiii*
Dedication .... *xv*
About the Author .... *xvii*

Chapter 1 .... *19*
Why Stay in College/University *19*
How to Pay For College/University *20*
The College Student's Pre-Check List *25*
Programs in Business Administration *27*
Rules of Surviva *28*
Other Rules *33*

Chapter 2 .... *35*
Managing our Money (Be Financially Savvy) *35*
Competencies For all Business and Non-Business Majors *36*
Curricula Patterns *38*
Choosing an Area of Emphasis *38*
Academic Requirements *39*
General Education and Grade requirements *39*
Minor Requirements *40*

Chapter 3 ... 41
Internships and Cooperative Programs ... 41
Business and Finance Lab ... 42
Graduation and Other Forms ... 42
Extra Curricular Activities ... 42

Chapter 4 ... 44
Effective Studying Habits ... 44
Examination Tips ... 46
Improving our Memory "Poor Memory is a Myth" ... 47
Memory Principles ... 48
Memory Skills ... 49

Chapter 5 ... 52
Career Preparations and Planning ... 52
Entrepreneurship ... 53
What If You Graduate From College / University ... 53
Sources of Job Opportunities ... 54
Graduate/Professional School ... 54
Business School Success Tips ... 56
Ten Tips on Filling Out the Business ... 57
Application Forms ... 57

Chapter 6 ... 58
Ten Tips on Succeeding in Business School ... 58
Ten Tips on Getting a Great Job After Business School ... 59
Job Opportunities for Business, Marketing, Finance, and Accounting ... 60

Suggestions For Taking Standardized Tests 61
Test taking Techniques – Answering Multiple 63
Choice Questions 63
Grades Grades Grades 65

Chapter 7 68
Goals of the Library Research Handbook 68
Citations Styles For Research Papers 69
Resume Preparations 71
The Cover Letter 75
The Resume format (Samples) 76
Cover Letter Format (Samples) 81

Chapter 8 84
The Interview Sessions 84
Positive Interview Tips 86
Tough Interview Questions 87
Questions You May Ask During Interview Sessions 89

Chapter 9 90
Twenty Five Reasons Why Applicants Don't Get the Job 90
Keeping the Job 92
Students – What Do Employers Expect of You 93

Success Stories 95
Conclusion 99

Preface and Acknowledgment

This Students' Survival Handbook is based on more than thirty years' experience as a Professor, Researcher, Entrepreneur, a Business/Educational Consultant, Business Department Chair, and Division Dean. It is also based on my training and preparations as an advisor and one who has guided the success of more than four thousand students from 1979 to 2014. It is further based on the work collaborated with Dr. Kojo Quartey- a noted professor, educator, and community servant in Talladega, Alabama. My hearty thanks go to the Dean of the Library, Mr. Heath at Stillman College, Tuscaloosa whose information and materials were very useful. I am especially grateful to Dr. McNealley, the President of Stillman College, Tuscaloosa, AL., and to Dr. Charlotte Carter for their leaderships that encouraged us to put in 150% of our time and efforts to insure the success of this unique institution – Stillman and the special Accreditation of the Business Programs. I am especially grateful to Dr. AL Ringleb, the Director of CIMBA Program in Paderno del Grappa, Italy and the University of Iowa, Iowa City, Iowa for according me the opportunity to serve as an Adj. Prof. of <u>Finance</u> during the Fall, 2011. The leadership program at CIMBA is an invaluable experience that enhances the quality of educational preparations of our future leaders.

The reader of this material is encouraged to use the section that pertains to his or her immediate need(s) as these include from pre-college preparations to first year of college/university to the final year in addition to what if after graduation and securing the job or going to professional school, what next?

To the Professor, this book contains basic facts that help you in your counseling sessions with student advisees as some of you may not have been trained as administrative educators in your capacity as educational consultants.

To the Students/parents and other readers, I am convinced that this College/University Survival Hand Book will answer many troubling and throbbing questions you may have.

It will also serve as a beneficial gift to your son, daughter, niece, nephew, uncle, relations and friends who are preparing to go to colleges or universities in addition to those who may not have an idea of what future may hold for them.

The author will be willing to respond to any questions the readers may have as he believes that the comprehensiveness of this hand book covers extensive areas that high school and university students will encounter. The email and phone numbers have been included to respond to any questions in either this or the second edition of the book.

Acknowledgments- the author wishes to use this opportunity to acknowledge his children – Dr. Chichi, Mr. Chike, and Ms. Chijiago Chijioke who some day will understand that fathers deserve to be loved too as Jesus loves us without being judgmental.

Dedication – this book is dedicated to my Late father – Chief Jonah Chijioke who sowed the seed of Love, hard work, and joy in his family. It is also dedicated to my beloved mother – Mrs. Hannah Chijioke who at the age of 104 has maintained the love of God to all men and women. May the abundance of Love and Blessing from God be with You in this and Life After.

Emmanuel M. Chijioke, MBA, Ph.D JD.
Prof. and Dean, Division of Business and SMI
P. O. Box 2453, Stillman College, Tuscaloosa, Al. 35403
echijioke@att.net or echijioke@stillman.edu
256 493 1237 or 205 366 8936

About the Author

Emmanuel M. Chijioke, MBA, Ph.D, JD is currently the Director of Bloomberg Information systems Initiative and Professor of Finance, Business, and Law at Stillman College, Tuscaloosa, AL. Dr. Chijioke started his Law Degree (JD) from Temple University School of Law in Philadelphia, PA and received it from Birmingham School of Law in Birmingham, AL, Ph. D from The University of Alabama, Tuscaloosa, AL, MBA and BS (Higher Honors) from Alabama A & M University, Normal, AL. He has in the last thirty (30) years served as a tenured Prof. of Finance, Business, and Law, Business Department Chair, and Business Division Dean. Dr. Chijioke owns and operates a Business and Educational Consulting Firm – CJ Associates and Investments. He has also served as a reviewer for the Academy of Management and the Academy of Legal Studies in Business to which he is also a professional member. He is an award winning fellow/visiting Professor at New York University, NY and a recipient of Hubert Hurst's Fellowship at the University of Florida, Gainesville, Florida. Dr. Chijioke recently served as Adjunct Professor of Finance for the University of Iowa, Iowa city, Iowa in Paderno Del Grappa, Italy under the auspices of CIMBA teaching abroad program. Dr. Chijioke is the author of three (3) books (In Progress) and has written and presented numerous articles in business, economics, law, and management in regional and national conferences and proceedings. Above all, he has utilized his training in education, evangelism business, and law in relating to and counseling more than four thousand students in the last thirty years.

Chapter 1

<u>*WHY STAY IN COLLEGE/UNIVERSITY?*</u> – While hundreds and thousands of people have been loosing their jobs over last year or more, only 2% of college graduates are unemployed. Here are some logical/good reasons why you should stay in College/University:

- Graduates with the Bachelor's degree earn 45% more annually than high school graduates
- Over a lifetime, individuals with the Bachelor's degree are projected to earn $2.1 million compared to $1.2 million for high school graduates
- College graduates have better housing options
- College graduates have greater access to quality healthcare
- They have more disposable income for vacation, hobbies, and leisure activities. With unemployment on the rise, companies are hiring only people with the training and skills necessary to contribute to the bottom line

- Government is promoting college education and is making it easier to pay for College by providing more financial aid.
- There is absolutely no reason for a student to stop out for financial reasons as there are many sources for financial support if the student is serious.

HOW TO PAY FOR COLLEGE/UNIVERSITY EDUCATION –

Sources of financial assistance for your academic programs include:

Federal Government – The Federal Government provides financial assistance to students in the form of grants and loans. Students and parents must apply for the assistance annually.

1. Grants – are free money awarded to students meeting certain requirements.
    - Federal Pell Grant – Available to all eligible students who have not received a Bachelor's degree
    - Federal Supplementary Educational Opportunity Grant (FSEOG) – Awarded to students who are Pell eligible with exceptional financial need.
    - SMART – Awarded to Pell eligible juniors and seniors who are Math or Science majors with a 3.0 GPA or higher.

- Academic Competitive Grant (ACG) – Awarded to Pell eligible freshmen and sophomores who have completed a rigorous Secondary School Program.
- TEACH – Provides grants up to $4000 per year to students who intended to teach in public or private elementary or secondary schools that serve students from low-income families.

2. Loans – Low interest loans provided through Direct Loans or Federal Family Education Loan Programs.
   The loans awarded to the student must be repaid starting with the seventh month after the student graduates from college. Parent loans must be repaid immediately.

- Stafford Subsidized loans – Loan awarded based on financial need.
- Stafford Unsubsidized loans – Loan is not based on financial need
- Parent Plus Loans – Parent Loan for undergraduate students (PLUS)
- Perkins Loans – College loans awarded directly to students who demonstrate financial need
- Private Loans – Terms for these loans vary by lender.

3. Work-Study Program – Provide employment opportunities for students while enrolled to help pay educational expenses.

State Governments – All state governments including the State of Alabama offer limited financial assistance to their residents who are attending private colleges. Students should contact the Financial Aid Office to obtain information about their grants opportunities.

- ATRIP – Alabama Teacher Recruitment Incentive Program. An eligible applicant must be a legal resident of Alabama enrolled as a full-time student in a teacher education program in the field of Mathematics, Special Education, General Science or English Language Arts.

  Alabama Student Grant – All Alabama residents are urged to apply for the Alabama Student Grant by providing five proofs of residency. This is a non-need base grant.

- Alabama Student Assistance – A grant program based on need and availability of funds is awarded only to Alabama residents with extremely limited resources.

Scholarships

1. Institutional Scholarship – The College awards different types of financial assistance to help students meet the cost of attendance. Students should seek information about types of institutional aid available from the Financial Aid Office.
2. UNCF Scholarships – The UNCF/College Fund offers over 450 types of scholarships, which have different requirements and deadlines. Students must see the Scholarship Managers to learn more about the different scholarships and how to apply for them.
3. Private Scholarships – There are numerous scholarships from Alumni, Corporations, and Philanthropic organizations that are available to students. The Scholarship Managers and alumni offices are available to assist students with the search for private and non-private scholarships in their chosen institutions.

Some capable parents may either pay or set up trust funds for their children's education. Sometimes the students parents' employers may contribute to or pay certain percent of their employees' children's education. If your parent or parents were to be professors, staff members or administrators at Colleges or Universities, they may earn partial or full tuition waivers for their children) at their colleges or universities.

If you are serious about available scholarships, work with your High School, Church or Community or Young men/women Christian Associations' counselors to work with you to prepare and save application letters about yourself for use when applying for college or university.

If you are serious about your education, you can enroll in College bound courses during your junior years in high school. This will enable you conclude your college degree in two and a half years and on to graduate school if you so choose or find a job.

If you are really serious, you can secure a job after high school with companies that reimburse your tuition such as "WallMart and Best Buy". Note that you must carefully plan, manage, and implement your timing very well.

You can choose to go to Oakwood University in Huntsville, Alabama, Loma-linda University in California, and Andrews University in Michigan or universities like them where you can work full time and take your classes. Here, you may not owe anything by the time you conclude your degree program.

Above all, you are encouraged to avoid any loans. Use it as the last resort knowing that any loans secured by students cannot be cancelled by bankruptcy proceedings.

The College Student's Pre-Check-List

Your check list begins with self evaluation of yourself called SWOT analysis. This is a process through which one examines his/her strengths (skills, intellect, social, and professional), weaknesses (that will make it difficult for achieving ones short range and long range goals), opportunities(that are within reach), and threats(that will obstruct your chances of achieving your strengths and opportunities).

— Devise personal strategies for containing and turning the weaknesses and threats into strengths.
— Additional check list for succeeding in colleges and universities are:
— Process of Registering for classes. Read instructions provided very carefully. Use counselors and advisors to help if you are lost.
— Checking into your dormitory or apartment or house
— Choosing a major- Be careful and understand that your major can determine your success or failure in life. Avoid easy majors as there are many students in that field thereby making job opportunities difficult.
— Managing your finances- Open checking and or savings' accounts on campus or off campus and manage them conservatively especially if you don't have a trust fund.

- Creating and managing your budget. Live within your means and conservatively.
- Building a good credit – Deposit $500.00 and borrow on it. Secure a loan for $500.00 based on the money you deposited, Leave the money in the bank and pay interest every month until the loan is paid off.
- Establish when to pay your bills every month but insure that the money is available for paying those bills when due.
- Establish when to visit your doctors for eye, health, and dental check ups once or twice in the year. Exercise as often as possible – two to three times a week.
- Keeping and maintaining personal and academic records at safe places.
- Locating campus or local resources
- Administrative offices, Post Office, Laundry, Business Offices, Registrar's Office, Police Department, and IT Department.
- Personal Safety- Roommate, Personal/Automobile Keys, and Automobile maintenance
- Emergency contact information(Telephone #s) – Parents, Brother/Sisters, and Campus Friends

PROGRAMS IN BUSINESS ADMINISTRATION

The Division of or Program in Business Administration is one of the unique divisions or programs in the College with students and faculty who aspire to be the best in all aspects of their endeavors.

This division or program grows by leaps and bounds and serves as the <u>cash</u> cow of the college or university. Currently, the major areas of study within most divisions are: Accounting, Management, Economics, Marketing, Finance and Legal Studies, Entrepreneurship, and Human Resources Management. A new interdisciplinary major in Sports Management has started attracting students attention to viable future field of specialization.

Concerted efforts are presently being made to revamp the business curriculum by providing more practically, technically, and entrepreneurially oriented courses and liberal arts options. Further information may be obtained from departmental offices.

On many occasions, our students get confused relative to many throbbing questions for which they may not have answered have answers and may not be willing to ask advisors, or school officials. At the same time, faculty and administrative personnel are hoping and seeking ways to. reach most of the students. Those students who are doing well are the ones who communicate with their advisors and other personnel while those who need the help more do not seek such help.

The author of this handbook has researched, gathered materials from several sources such as the University of Alabama, Tuscaloosa, AL., Alabama A. & M. University, Normal, AL., Temple University, Philadelphia, PA., New York University, New YorK, NY., Northwest University, Evanston, ILL., Harvard University, Boston, MA., Talladega College, Talladega, AL., and Stillman College, Tuscaloosa, AL in his professional development classes, traditional, and non-traditional classes including consultations at the Federal Corrections Institute and Anniston Army Depot in the last thirty (30)years.

The author hopes that this STUDENT SUCCESS SURVIVAL HANDBOOK will achieve the intended objectives ie for the reader to surmount most of the obstacles associated with College/university programs, prepare for the next stage in his/her life, and make a difference in his/her College family, real world family, and the Society at large.

RULES OF SURVIVAL

During your tenure in higher education, you will be given extensive advices on how to negotiate through your college years and beyond. Some of these may be worthwhile, others may not be so sound. In an attempt to provide you with survival techniques for your years in college and beyond, the following rules of survival are those which, if adhered to and applied wisely, would maximize the probability of your successfully surviving the four (more or less) years of college and the years that follow – either in graduate/professional school or in the work force.

These rules are sound solid suggestions. They are as follows:

A. Take Responsibility for Your Actions and Performances: the most critical component of survival in the "game of life" is the simple one of accepting the principal responsibility for your fate. Do not blame others for your shortcomings as "Life is what you make it." While there may be a variety of factors beyond your control, in the final analysis, your fate rests in your hands. DO NOT EXPECT OTHERS TO TAKE CARE OF YOU.

While the faculty, staff, and administrators are here to assist, enlighten, and facilitate your educational and life pursuit, you must know and abide by the rules, procedures, and policies that will ultimately determine your fate in life.

B. Challenge Yourself: Realize that education is a learning process and keep a positive attitude, realizing that if you believe in God and in yourself, you can do almost anything. Excelling in every course demand challenging yourself, believing, and working hard smartly.

While challenging yourself, take a variety of courses in Mathematics, Computer Applications, Logics, Critical Thinking, Arts and Sciences and some courses in Unconventional areas such as Music, Philosophy, Strategic Management, and Service Marketing—these should help make you a well Rounded Educated person.

Remember why you are here — to become a well rounded educated person, not simply for a degree.

C. Ask Questions:

Remember that the only stupid question is the one that is not asked. If you do not understand anything, ask questions. Do not be afraid of appearing stupid.

Asking questions is a part of the learning process to which you have paid and deserve to be encouraged by the response.

D. Know and Use your Advisor(s)

All students have academic advisors. If you do not know your advisor, consult with your department chair or division dean. Your advisor is here to help you. If you have any problems, do not hesitate to contact your advisor, the department chair or the dean of your division.

Note that helping you is one of his/her jobs. Be honest with your advisor otherwise he/she may find it hard to trust and help you.

E. Manage your Time Wisely

While in college, remember that your most precious resource is probably time. Prioritize your activities and maintain a schedule. Use time between classes to study. If you manage your time wisely, you may even excel at your studies while maintaining a full or part time job.

F. Enjoy your Education

Do not attempt to make life anymore complicated than it is, as long as you adhere to the rules of any organization and learn to conform, you will survive. Even if you decide to challenge any rules, handle it with dignity, respect and care after having done your research for logical reasons for challenging such rules.

Talk to your advisor first and hear him/her out before going further.

While in college, there are courses (and even professors) that you will like and those you will not like. Learn to appreciate that which you abhor and enjoy that which you relish. If you dislike all the courses in your major, you are obviously in the wrong major and this will be reflected in your grades; you may need to change your major. No matter your circumstance, enjoy your college education as it will be the best period in your life and a true learningexperience.

G. *Never Miss Class Without Very Good Reasons*

You have paid for your education. Do not miss classes. Treat your classes like important business meetings. Each day you miss class you deduct $1,000 from your Life earnings. If you cannot make it to class, make sure you have a valid written excuse.

Endeavor to contact a friend or the professor to find out what you missed. Borrow your friend's note book if you trust his/her ability to take good notes. Remember that these notes may contain some of the questions that may appear on your test.

Some times, the Professor's Assistant may help especially if he/she had taken such course.

H. <u>Do Not Associate with the Wrong Crowd</u>

Do not associate with negative people or individuals who steer you in the wrong direction. If people you associate with are low achievers, beware.

Associate with those who exert a positive influence on your education and life. Don't be at the wrong places at the wrong time.

I. <u>Other Rules</u>

   - adhere to all deadlines – No excuses,

- create a portfolio for safe keeping copies of all papers and documents for your records
- keep copies of your transcripts
- failure is not and can never be an option
- use or consult your tutors when necessary
- learn to obey rules and conform as you would wish for others to obey the rules you establish as a leader
- use a dictionary and thesaurus if necessary.
- Use your computer for grammar and spell check.
- do all your work neatly
- get used to using the computer for your work and projects
- try to get along with your professors, administrators, and students
- try to always look your best – always dress responsibly and for the occasion

The above rules of survival are by-no-mean comprehensive in nature. They are provided to help you succeed during and after college days. The most important key to excellence in college, is the desire to go the extra mile and to challenge yourself by pushing yourself to a higher level of satisfactory limit.

Chapter 2.

Managing Your Money: "Be Financially Savvy"

The game of being financially savvy includes and not limited to:
- *Living within your means*
- *Don't borrow money you can't afford to pay back at least by the end of the month*
- *Limit the number of credit and debit cards to 2 each. Use them on emergency situations*
- *If possible, use family plan cell phone with limited or unlimited minutes*
- *BE Drug Free – Use prescribed medications accordingly*
- *Do not misuse your work study/financial aid funds*
- *If you live off-campus, insure that you pay your rent on time every month or preferably one semester or a year if you can afford it*
- *Work hard to secure a scholarship or scholarships through academics, sports, or a combination*

- Avoid vacations that are costly and not well planned in advance
- Avoid emergency travels that can be avoided or postponed

COMPETENCIES FOR ALL BUSINESS ADMINISTRATION AND NON-BUSINESS MAJORS

Students, regardless of major, should possess the following general competencies:

(1) interpersonal skills

(2) technical and theoretical skills

(3) communication skills

Interpersonal skills are a must for anyone who seeks to function effectively in the world of business. All students who matriculate from either the Business Division or College or school are expected to possess excellent interpersonal skills. These skills include the ability to get along well with others, interviewing skills, and job retention skills. The Division provides seminars and tips on these skills in the classroom. These skills deal with the student's knowledge of the underlying theory necessary to function effectively in any professional environment. Emphasis is not only on knowledge learned in the classroom but on the application of the in-class knowledge to real world experiences. These include knowledge of basic accounting, economics, finance, computers and all business-related subjects. In light of this, the principles' courses (management, accounting, finance, economics and marketing are required for all business majors). Projects in a number of classes, internships and co-operative programs provide invaluable experiences. You must also learn how to think critically. The Bloomberg Information system is a tool for you to learn and gain experience in the workings and discussions of the stock market and financial analyses.

Computers are an integral part of all courses. The Business and Finance Lab will give you the opportunity to integrate your theoretical knowledge with computer applications.

Effective communication skills – both written and oral expressions are indispensable to any professional. It is particularly important to those working with the customers and the public. You must consistently communicate information to others. You should be able to write business letters, memoranda, etc very well.

You must also be an effective speaker. Many Instructors are required to incorporate writing, reading, and speaking assignment into each class. So, just enjoy good communication in all your classes. Those who obtain degrees in Business Administration should also possess skills in the following areas: General Education, Accounting, Economics, Communications, Behavioral Sciences, Computers, Research capability, Mathematics, Statistics, Applied Business Administration courses, and Feasibility study.

Graduates with Business Administration or related degrees should possess the foundation for lifelong learning, development, and growth. The trust of the business programs is to train students to become entrepreneurs and future leaders. You are encouraged to mesh any field of study with computer application skills.

CURRICULA PATTERNS

The curricula patterns below should provide you with the information you need. This should coincide with your college or university catalog.

Adhere to this, remembering that you do not exactly have to take courses in a particular sequence. In any case, confer with your advisor before taking any courses as there are necessary prerequisites for taking certain Business courses.

CHOOSING AN AREA OF EMPHASIS

While trying to decide on your area of emphasis, remember the basic rules of supply and demand. There is serious saturation in the job market for subject areas that are easy especially those that are not mathematically challenged. The demand in the job market is always open for those fields that are difficult especially those that are mathematically challenged such as Accounting, Finance/Banking, Operations' Management, Economics, and Statistics.

Internship opportunities are available to those who major in challenging fields. Therefore, think seriously before making such choice unless you have the family connections where the doors will always be open no matter what degree to which you majored.

ACADEMIC REQUIREMENTS

Academic requirements include the general education requirements (for all students regardless of major) and major requirements.

These will be listed and discussed for all Business Administration majors with your major advisors (Accounting, Economics, and Management), Finance and Banking major, and the Public Administration major. In addition, a listing of all the courses is again provided in the catalog.

General Education and Grade Requirements

These are courses that all students, regardless of major must take. Most of these courses are, however, non-business courses. A student who earns an 'F' grade in any of these courses must repeat in order to graduate. Although, a grade of 'D' is not subject to be repeated, students are encouraged to repeat all courses with 'D' grades. Note all major courses with D grades must be taken over with a C or higher grade before graduation.

MINOR REQUIREMENTS

Students may obtain a minor in any field with eighteen credit hours within the department by choosing any combination of business courses, including those listed in the catalog. Business Administration majors may also obtain a minor from other departments by completing a minimum of 18 credit hours in the department in question.

Students are encouraged to consider minoring in Computer Science, Operations Management, Psychology, Communications, Finance, Entrepreneurship, Marketing, and Mathematics. Consult with your advisor and the appropriate department.

Chapter 3

INTERNSHIPS & CO-OPERATIVE PROGRAMS

Make sure you sign up early for internships and or cooperative programs. The Placement Office, the Business, Finance Programs, and your advisor can help you with this.

You may stop by the Business and Finance Lab to receive help with your resume' and application. These are forms that need to be completed prior to your going on a co-op or internship assignment.

Make sure you secure approval of the department chair, your advisor, and the co-op office. You will have to complete all forms and a report or term paper in order to earn credits. Only your co-op advisor in the department and the supervisor at the work place will be responsible for assigning your grade and credits. If you do not sign up prior to your co-op assignment, you may not receive any credit.

BUSINESS AND FINANCE LAB

The Business and Finance Lab and Resource Centers are for your use. They will provide information on various subjects as well as computer assistance for your classes and tutorial assistance in any field, not just business. Take advantage of the lab, its tutors, and other facilities.

GRADUATION AND OTHER FORMS

Check with your advisor and the Registrar's office for the various forms you will need to fill out prior to graduation in addition to surveys for improving the offerings. Keep copies of all forms you turn in. Meet with the Institutional Bursar or the Business Office to confirm your financial balance. If you are owing any money, begin early to find the source to settle this debt knowing that you may not receive your diploma when you are ready to graduate.

EXTRA-CURRICULAR ACTIVITIES

Several organizations exist within the Division of Business Administration and on campus. These include The Students in Free Enterprise (SIFE), Delta Sigma Lamda, and others. These organizations take trips to various places and participate in Community activities. SIFE participates in an Annual Regional Competition based on projects it completed during the season. You are encouraged to join these organizations as they will add value to your resume.

ENACTUS   ENACTUS   ENACTUS

Chapter 4

EFFECTIVE STUDYING HABITS

There are certain things you can do to give yourself a better chance to receive the highest grade possible in your class.

1. Go to all classes; "If you're there, they will care."
2. Manage you time wisely; "Time is money."
3. Get to know your professors early. Ask them questions after class early in the semester.
4. Sit in the front and pay attention
5. Discuss possible extra credit early in the semester: NOT LATER!
6. Make them aware of your unexcused absences
7. Use your department advisor! He/she can save you time and help you with another professor where necessary. Visit them.
8. Start notebooks early in the semester. Set them up neatly… organize them well…put in them exactly what is asked for.

9. Be on time for class.
10. When using tutors, take to them questions or problems you have already gone over...don't go to them cold! Use them well. Take all out-of-class papers and projects to them to double check and have them advise you.
11. Take good notes in class: don't write stories; abbreviate and use numbers; keep all notes from one class in order and in one notebook for each class.
12. If possible, record classes on tape. This is another good way to study. Note that it must be approved by the professor and students.
13. RECOPY NOTES EVERY NIGHT. THIS IS THE BEST WAY TO STUDY. Clean them up and make them neat! Recopying notes is a great way to study for a test.
    Don't just sit there and stare at a book. TAKING NOTES ARE THE KEY TO SUCCESS.
14. Express serious interest at all times and stay interested.
15. Ask professors for help...you can make friends with good ones!
16. <u>Read</u> in quiet places at quiet times if possible. If you can read with music on, good for you. If you can read with a headset in a noisy environment, so be it.
17. Study <u>notes</u> for tests or a combination of notes and books before a test.

18. Use loud time to recopy notes, make lists for classes, put together notebooks for classes, work on projects, etc.
19. When you read, take very brief notes on what you read and you may never have to go back to the book.
20. Make <u>lists</u> of people, places, rules, things, dates, formulas, etc., to study for your tests. Lists are easy to use to see exactly what you know and what you need to work on.
21. Participate in class discussions. Ask questions and get your professors to know who you are early in the semester

EXAMS TIPS

1. Read questions carefully.
2. Think carefully before you answer a question.
3. Write neatly, legibly, and thoroughly.
4. Be mindful of the allotted time and work with it.

5. Use the entire exam period for the exam.
6. Check all your answers.

IMPROVING YOUR MEMORY "POOR MEMORY IS A MYTH"

No one has a weak memory, even when you are frustrated with your studies. Note that memory is a mental activity where information is impressed either faintly or strongly in your nervous system.

Each person has the capacity to organize and direct his/her mental activity or remembering, to make strong impression called "neural traces"

You can remember better if you follow these "Four R's of Remembering"

Resolve: Develop a serious intention to remember the lectures or what you read in your textbook. Avoid focusing on your emotions and mental conditions. Just try to remember the information through focusing on the subject matter rather than on yourself. Research says that one of the most important factors in a memory is the "predisposition to remember."

React: Your mental activity is very active when you focus on what you wish to remember. Think about it, make a picture of it mentally, write it down, generate a feeling (emotional response) to it, talk it over (to self or others), or apply it practically to daily life activities.

Reflect: Think deeply about the information you wish to remember. Associate the new idea or fact with something you already know about and are interested in. Make an analogy (comparison of similar ideas) between your subject and what you already know.

For example – a tomato is a fruit, connect this with all you know about fruits. The more interest you develop about the tomato as a fruit, it creates the curiosity to learn more and remember it as a "fruit."

Refresh: Brush up on your memories as soon as you learn new information. Review immediately to make it stronger "neural traces" or "information impressions" in your brain. Repetition on daily, weekly, and monthly basis is the key to not forgetting the brushed up information by the end of the semester.

<u>Memory Principles</u>

1. Intend to remember/learn/study
2. Get an "overview" of the task
3. Review immediately after learning
4. Learn activity
5. Use an hour or two to learn

6. Practice what you have learned
7. Learn in an organized way
8. Set and understand the goals/objectives for your study

Memory Skills: Source: The University of Alabama Learning Skills Center(1989)

Recalling information or what you have read is based on the following memory skills:

1. *What we Intended to Remember:* We tend to learn in accordance with how much interest, incentive, and intention we have in learning.

   At the same time, we remember those things that we are motivated to remember, whether we are naturally interested or have created an interest and enthusiasm in learning the subject matter because we realize the ultimate benefits. Intended to remember is perhaps the most vital learning task.

2. Selectively Choose Memory Tasks: No one can remember everything he/she has heard or seen. Selecting the important topics, facts, and ideas and disregarding the least essential elements allows for maximum memory to occur. Therefore, when studying, first skim the chapter outline to identify key concepts to be remembered.

3. Understand the Material: A poorly understood concept is difficult to remember because it has little meaning. For long term recall, it is necessary to understand what you are trying to remember.

4. Review: Immediate review (after class lectures or textbook reading), even if for a few minutes, reinforces learning and remembering of materials. The greatest amount of forgetting occurs directly after finishing the learning task(psychologists say within 20 minutes). Try reviewing notes immediately before and after class periods to enhance recall.

5. Use All of Your Senses: The gift of Sight and Hearing are the most important senses in acquiring information. While both need to be used, choose which one is more comfortable for you (Visual or Auditory learning). For both styles, mental recitation is important in transferring material from short-term to long term memory. Experts suggest that 80% of textbook study should be involved in reciting and 20% in reading.

6. Associate New Materials with Prior Knowledge: Learn new materials by associating the new idea with something you already know about and are interested in. As new learning occurs with your later courses, this material will provide additional background with associated

future learning. Note, the more you learn, the easier it is to learn more because you have a broader base for anchoring new information.

7. Use Short Study Periods Rather Than Cramming: As a general rule, short study periods meshed with rest intervals are to be preferred over massed practice or cram sessions. The exception to this rule would involve the writing of a paper where organizational tasks would require longer work periods and more intense concentrations on the project without break.

8. Organize Materials Meaningfully: Large masses of materials are less threatening and more easily committed to memory when broken into smaller sections, and then relate the sections to each other

9. Learning By Association: The use of Mnemonic devices can be helpful. This may include phrases or combinations or words that could be associated and adapted to material to be remembered, but mnemonic devices could be used only until you know the material so well that you no longer need them.

THESE PRINCIPLES SHOULD HELP YOU IMPROVE YOUR MEMORY DURING STUDY PERIODS.

Chapter 5

CAREER PREPARATION AND PLANNING

While in college, you need to be thinking about professional or graduate schools and/or work upon graduation. College is designed to prepare you for what lies ahead.

In line with this, the author has provided this section on job preparations, interviewing techniques, resume preparation, and how to keep a job. It amounts to surviving after the college years are over.

Remember, that whether you are a freshman, sophomore, junior, or a senior, you need to prepare a resume to identify where you are, your accomplishments, and where you hope to be in the next few years.

ENTREPRENEUSHIP

Understanding that at one time or another in your life, you would like to start and operate your own business. You are therefore, encouraged to:

- Attend all seminars on how to start a business
- Join some of the students-run businesses or projects such as (Chocolate, Cake, Doughnut, Valentine Baskets, etc.)
- Attend as many seminars as possible
- Sign up for internship, co-op, and apprenticeship programs for needed experience

What If You Graduate From College/University: What next?

— Go back to your SWOT analysis
— Where are you today – What strengths and skills have you acquired in the last 3 or 4 years

- Determine your realistic and practical job options
- Develop appropriate marketing plan to address the feasible job options
- Implement the marketing plan that address each of the needs of the prospective employer

Sources of job opportunities:

- Internship or Cooperative job experience while in School
- Bloomberg Corporate Information Sources
- Employment Agencies(Federal, State, County, City, Profit and Non-Profit Agencies)
- Local and National Newspapers
- Internet Searches
- Check the Moody's Industrials for corporations and jobs
- Check with local and regional libraries.

If You Choose to Go to Graduate/Professional Schools:

GRADUATE/PROFESSIONAL SCHOOL

University & College- Students' Successful Survival Handbook

This is probably the only time that Clem's name and the title 'Ph.D' will be used in the same sentence.

Think GMAT, LSAT, and GRE during junior years or early in your senior year (check with the lab for preparation material and help and attend all preparation sessions). Apply to graduate school early. Apply for financial aid earlier. Get recommendations from reliable individuals. Research the schools and narrow your choices down to a few — all of different levels — at least one top-notch, one above-average and one average. Consider schools with an MBA/Law Program. Graduate schools are looking for the following qualities:

1. High Academic Ability — Grade point average, High GMAT, GRE, or LSAT scores
2. Leadership involvement — contributions to organizations as indication of leadership.
3. Work Experience — sign of maturity and experience — this includes internships and coop programs.

4. Express unique qualities – breath and types of courses taken (diversification); Math, Economics, and statistics courses; letter of interest; background; determination.

BUSINESS SCHOOL TIPS

Ten tips on getting into Good Business Schools:
1. Make sure that business school is right for you.
2. Get as much information as possible on the schools to which you are applying.
3. Build up your college grade point average to a minimum of 3.25 average.
4. Study for the Graduate Management Admissions Test (GMAT) or GRE.
5. Get a solid grounding in Math, Economics, Statistics, and English.
6. Pursue leadership roles in college and community activities
7. Apply early. You don't have to pay any money. Know what your test's score were to be before you decide to send any money.
8. Use any connections you have (Established Pastors, Lawyers, Congressmen/women, Senators, Business Presidents/CEOs for letters of recommendation).
9. Work for one to two to three or to four years before you apply to graduate business schools. Since your graduate

schoolwork will be based on the practical job you did with your business.

10. Make the most of whatever opportunity you have in college or on a summer or regular job.

Ten Tips on Filling Out the Business School Application Forms

1. Market yourself as a valuable addition to any MBA program.
2. Be aggressive in both style and content.
3. Identify what you have done that is unusual, unique, or outstanding.
4. Be justifiably proud of your accomplishments.
5. Communicate that you are right for the school and the school is right for you.
6. Keep essays short, interesting, and to the point (see advisor for samples).
7. Make the application look professional–typed, neat, and error free (have your Advisor read it).
8. Use professional References or recommendations.
9. Take your time and take it seriously.
10. Be honest and candid.

Chapter 6

Ten Tips on Succeeding in Business Schools

1. Be aggressive and take the initiative
2. Learn to manage you time. Don't fall behind in your work.
3. Form study groups especially in mathematically oriented courses.
4. Get to know your classmates both academically and socially.
5. Take advantage of the opportunity to know and work with faculty (Work on their projects).
6. Know where to get help if you need it.
7. Get involved in school clubs and activities.
8. Learn to Write and speak clearly, concisely, and logically.
9. Think conceptually, critically, and practically.
10. Keep it all in perspective.

Ten Tips on Getting a Great Job after Business School

1. Determine what you feel will be a great job for you. Conduct personal SWOT analysis (Personal strengths, weaknesses, opportunities, and threats).
2. Interview with carefully chosen companies to learn what is available and what is best for you.
3. Experiment with a summer job in an industry that interest you.
4. Take full advantage of the school's recruiting facilities and programs.
5. Use whatever contacts/networks at your reach.
6. Write a resume that highlights your achievements.
7. Be knowledgeable before the interview about the company, its markets, products/services, and industry trends.
8. Don't go only for the money. Keep in mind Flexibility, future opportunity, and personal fit with the company.
9. Be aggressive and confident.
10. Be persistent but know when to contain your self

JOB OPPORTUNITIES FOR BUSINESS, MARKETING, FINANCE AND ACCOUNTING

Accounting, International Business Advertising, Banking (loans, credit dept.), and etc.

Investment and Job Analyst, Insurance, Budget

Accounting, Forensic Accounting, and Human Resources Management.

Business Planning, Communications, Loan Administration

Community Relations, Marketing and Merchandising

Consumer Research, Manufacturing, Comptrollership

Military Service, Controllership, New Business Research

Counseling, Operating Plans and Procedures

Credit Analysis, Operations Management, Customer Relations and Services, Operations Research Analysts

Data Processing and Programming, Organizational planning

Economic Analysts and Econometrics Personnel

Industrial Relations, social Services, Transportation

Forecasting Placement, Education (Teaching) Plant Protection

Employee Relations, Politics (Congressional aide, etc.)

Federal Government, Public Relations, Finance

Economic Development Enterprise Studies

Staff Accounting Forensic Accounting

SUGGESTIONS FOR TAKING STANDARDIZED TESTS

By Preston Rowe, MS- Comp. Sc. & Ph. D., Prof. of Psychology and Computational Sciences and Emmanuel Chijioke, Ph.D. JD Prof. of Finance and Law

Spend some of your preparation time considering not only rules, definitions and formulas, but also general properties that are often used in items, such as: even powers are always positive, positive powers of any value, but when the value is between zero and one, its powers are less than the value itself.

- Review knowledge as <u>systems</u> known as sets of facts
- There are some ideas one is expected to know:
    About transaction of parallel lines
    About similar geometric figures
    About right triangles
- Review arithmetic of fractions and signed number
- Look for key, handle, translation, trick that makes the path to the solutions obvious; many are like that
- If your approach requires a lot of calculations, it is undoubted on the wrong track
- Postponing calculation often saves time; for example, leaving 17/18 in fraction form would pay off if the next step were to multiply the fraction by 54/34 (the product reduces to 1/6)
- Invest in planning a solution before diving into particular calculations

Before the exam, practice writing down the steps needed to solve the problem (without actually executing them); you need to cultivate awareness of when to do what and why (Don't wing it!)

The information in many problems can be organized in several ways, only some of which can be useful; practice mental reorganizing. For examples, tables can be a sequence of rows or a sequence of columns; what is primary or in the center of attention can be made secondary and something else be the focus

- It helps to concretize problems: make useful sketches so that your eye-brain can see patterns; create a specific example from an abstract description. For example, "the sum of three consecutive numbers" can be illustrated as 1+2+3=6" and "2+3+4=9" and "3+4+5=12"; (incidentally, concerning building a knowledge of number properties, do you notice any pattern emerging from just looking at these three examples?)
- The Pythagorean theorem is almost always concretized as 3-4-5 or 5-12-13, as these are the only cases that are simple to calculate
- Watch out for some simple, but confusing algebraic properties, such as (a+b)x(a+b) = (a+b)(a+b) = ? There must be some storing up of isolated rules, details, etc., but avoid memorizing; understanding through seeing relations and patterns is the best way to assure future usefulness
- When practicing exams, do them under time pressure to get used to the pace; but also return to them as if you had all the time in the world and think of better ways to solve them (it's like Monday morning quarterbacking)

Test-Taking Techniques: Answering Multiple-Choice Questions

1. Thoroughly prepare — study, study, study!!!
2. Read, understand and carefully follow all directions.
3. Preview the entire exam before beginning.
4. Answer easy questions first

5. Attempt every question.
6. Think about what you know and answer the questions before reading the options.
7. Consider all alternatives and select the broadcast, most comprehensive answer.
8. Your first hunch is usually a good one—DO NOT change answers unless you are sure about the second choice.
9. Read each choice as a true or false item, eliminating False options.
10. `Look for qualifiers—note if the question asks for first, initial or best response.
11. Always, all, never and none are absolutes and are rarely correct.
12. Wrong choices <u>tend</u> to be either very brief or very long and involved.
13. Read the question carefully to see if a <u>negative verb</u> is used.
14. When included as a choice "all of the above/none of the above" is correct about <u>60%</u> of the time.
15. Identify <u>key issue</u> concerns in any answer options.
16. Eliminate the response that may be best for a decision-maker to make.

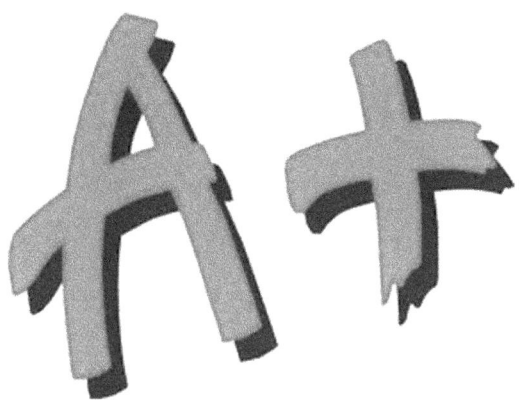

GRADES... GRADES... GRADES

ESTABLISH PRIORITIES, SET HIGH GOALS (SHORT & LONG TERM).

VALUE WHAT YOU LEARN, ELIMINATE DISTRACTIONS, SOLVE LIFE PROBLEMS

RESTRUCTURE TIME AS NECESSARY, AVOID OVER COMMITMENTS

YOU ARE RESPONSIBLE FOR WHAT YOU LEARN.

ORGANIZE YOUR STUDY AND YOUR TIME VERY WELL

NEAT WORK CAN IMPROVE YOUR GRADE, WORK CAREFULLY & THOROUGHLY.

ELIMINATE CRAMMING, STUDY SOMETHING EVERY DAY.

CULTIVATE A POSITIVE ATTITUDE.

ALWAYS GO TO CLASS AND SIT UP FRONT.

NAME ACCOMPLISHMENTS AT THE END OF THE DAY OR WEEK.

MAKE UP MISSED WORK/CORRECT ERRORS, STAY MOTIVATED

ALLOW SELF TO MAKE ERRORS, UNDERSTAND THE ERRORS AND CORRECT THEM. KEEP STANDARDS HIGH AND DON'T SETTLE FOR C OR D WORK.

EVALUATE PROGRESS AT REGULAR INTERVALS

ASK QUESTIONS TO REVIEW WHAT YOU'VE LEARNED.

NEVER NEGLECT TO USE INSTUCTORS AS A RESOURCE.

DILIGENT PREPARATIONS = "A" GRADES.

Electronic Appliances: Lap top, Cell Phones, I-Pads, I-Phones & Other Consult with your instructor to seek permission before you can introduce any of the electronic appliances in the class room as many professors are uncomfortable if students choose to introduce them without permission. In many cases, the syllabus specifically states if such is allowed or not. So read and consult with the instructor to insure clear communication.

Chapter 7

GOALS OF THE LIBRARY RESEARCH HANDBOOK

Using this handbook, faculty and students can learn how to access all of the resources of the William H. Sheppard and other Libraries to conduct research for papers, articles, thesis, and essays. We are blessed to have the Bloomberg Financial Information Systems in the Library to facilitate financial and economic researches. With the help of your instructors and the library staff, the following will be easy:

— Learning how to use the Internet and wide variety of electronic information services available through the Library to research information needed in your classes and that you will eventually need for your senior thesis.

— Accessing books that are contained within the Library and with the help of your instructors access books available through inter-library loans and from the libraries of the University Of Alabama and Shelton State Community College.

— Gaining access to information available through the various reference works and indexes available in this and other regional and national Libraries.

— Gaining access to information in videotapes and other media material and equipment both to research all academic fields and to make presentations in classes both to research all academic fields and to make presentations in classes or for the presentation of your senior thesis.

— Learning to assess the reliability of information presented through all of the facilities of the library so as to use it effectively for class assignments and you senior thesis.

Citation Styles For Research Papers

Of the Three major publication style manuals which should you use? Ask each of your advisors which style he or she wants you to use. If he or she has no preference, you can use one of these guidelines:

— APA: psychology, education, and other social sciences http://owl.english.purdue.edu/owl/resource/560/01/ REF/B76.7/.A46 This is used more by social scientists and business writers.

- MLA: Literature, arts, and humanities http://owl.english.purdue.edu/owl/resource/557/01/   REF/LB2369/.G53 This is used more by those in literature, communications, arts, humanities.
- Turabian: designed for college students to use with all subjects

  http://www.itaca.edu/library/course/turabian.html

- Business students and faculty use this more than any other disciplines.

  Automated Catalog

- Books in the Sheppard or other Libraries are found by searching the Online Public Access Catalog (OPAC). The OPAC's are accessible on each floor in the library, two in the lobby on the first floor, one in each of the rooms on the mezzanine floor, and one on the second floor in the periodicals room. The automated catalog is also accessible on the Internet at http://www.stillman.edu/stillman/library/library.html

RESUME PREPARATION

The resume is an essential part of a job search campaign. A resume is, in short, a Written Summary that gives an employer a preliminary impression of you by indicating your interests, education, work experience and personal background. In addition, a resume is a sample of your ability to organize and express yourself in writing.

Careful planning and preparations are necessary prerequisites for a clear, concise, complete resume.

Before you write your resume, you should have a clear understanding of who you are and what you have to offer

No one can write a resume that is exactly like another person's because each person must build upon his own experience.

First, honestly and thoroughly assess yourself in relation to your work and educational experiences with particular emphasis on your motivations, goal(s), strengths, weaknesses, likes and dislikes.

Evaluate yourself in terms of what you have accomplished. Compile a list of your skills and experiences–all of them- even those you don't think matter at all.

This inventory will help you pick and choose the most relevant aspects of your background to use in constructing an interesting, comprehensive, yet superior resume.

For example, did you work to help pay your way through college?

What jobs did you hold? How were they obtained? How many hours a week did you work? What did you enjoy most and like least about your work assignments?

What about extracurricular campus activities? Were the activities or your role in them indications of professional and personal interests and traits? Did you choose to be active in a group related to your field of study? This shows professional orientation. Did you hold and office in one of these organizations? This is a sign of potential leadership qualities.

What skills do you have? Identity two or three of your major skills which are highly related to the type of work you would like to do.

For what does your education qualify you? Consider functional areas in various types of businesses; e.g., government, industry, etc.

Do you have any special talents, aptitudes, limitations? Have you received any scholarships or awards? Analyze personal abilities, talents and interests correctly and stress the strong points as they relate to the type of work being sought.

Following your self-analysis, you need to decide on the format for you resume. There is no generalized "best" resume format.

Conciseness, organization, physical appearance and presentation sequence count when your resume competes for attention with other resumes. Your objectives, education and experiences will dictate the best order of presentation and emphasis.

When you search for a job, you are competing against many other people. For that reason, your resume must project you as being different from all other applicants and better suited to do the job.

Make your layout easy to read by leaving sufficient space between categories and underlining and/or capitalizing major items and headings. Your use of space is most important in creating and impression of neatness and orderliness. Space can be used to isolate important points to which you want to draw attention.

Long complex sentences and lengthy paragraphs leave a blurred image or none at all. Keep sentences down to ten to twelve words and paragraphs down to three or four lines. Resume content is very important, so carefully justify every work, sentence and paragraph. Length may vary, but as a general rule, the resume should be no more than two pages in length.

Once you have written the rough draft of your resume, you will need to make corrections, additions and deletions before it is ready for duplication.

Have you checked for spelling and grammatical errors? <u>A **_resume must be error free!_**</u> Is the document attractive? Do your margins offer enough space to facilitate easy reading? Most importantly, does the resume reflect you?

This individual will check for errors that you overlooked and can possibly give you suggestions for improvement.

Always use a computer and save your resume as well as cover letter on your fly drive or the clouds. Note that your work study at the College is an integral part of your resume and should be included. Unless your performance was less than encouraging for your supervisor to be uncomfortable talking about it. Insure to save different versions of your resume on a fly drive or disk or the clouds.

After your resume has been prepared, you will want to do some research on various companies. Information gathered through research will help you protect your own interests and match your qualifications and career objective realistically with specific companies. You should find out:

- the number of years each company has been in business
- where its plants, offices or stores are located
- what its products or services are
- what its growth has been and how its prospects look for the future
- what its summarized financial outlook reveals

Your research may lead you to contact a company directly to find out if they have career information available. Many companies publish brochures designed specifically to help guide you in applying your skills to particular job areas.

The Cover Letter

The cover letter is an important part of the resume package you submit to a prospective employer. An effective cover letter should add to your resume. Both should contribute to your professional image and be an expression of your written communications and organizational skills.

The cover letter should be three or four paragraphs in length and may be prepared according to the sample format provided in this handbook. If you want to vary certain information to fit individual companies, this can be done in a cover letter rather than in the resume.

After you have composed the letter, proofread it. Correct all spelling and grammatical errors. You should type your letter on business stationery that matches your resume stationery. Do not mimeograph a single form letter for mass distribution to many companies. Each cover letter should be tailored to fit an individual company and position. Do not address your letter to "To Whom It May Concern." Make the effort to discover who is responsible for hiring activities and direct your letter to that person.

Proofread your typed letter and have someone else proofread it for typographical errors, Retype the letter if you find errors.

Spell and grammar checking computerized system will be ideal

Resume Format (sample)

The following format illustrates the recommended form and content for your resume. The use of indentation, underlining and broad headings allow the employer to make an initial evaluation of you credentials in relation to specific job openings in a short amount of time.

YOUR NAME
PRESENT ADDRESS PERMANENT ADDRESS
Street
City, State Zip Code City, State Zip Code
Phone

PROFESSIONAL OBJECTIVE(S) Describe that type of work you desire, both a short-range and on a long range basis.

EDUCATION Present highest degree data first, and work backward. Identify: Major, minor, courses of study, institution granting degree and Date(s) of graduation.

EXPERIENCE Identify employer, your title and a brief description of the duties (Consider the one that reflects the job for which you are apply)

(DATE) performed. Start with the most recent employment and record data in reverse chronological order.

(DATE) Include volunteer work without pay if the work is related to the Professional objective. Also include summer jobs of significant Duration and importance.

HONORS AND Include clubs, organizations, and honor societies. If an officer, include ACTIVITIES specify which office.

SPECIAL SKILLS Special skills (knowledge of computers, software and hardware, ACTIVITIES office machines, etc.) and hobbies; travel, knowledge of other Countries, language, etc.

MILITARY SERVICE If applicable, include the branch of service, dates of service, rate or Rank, and experience.

REFERENCES Include at least 3 current references with emails and phone numbers

Sample Resume for JOHN Doe

<u>Permanent Address</u> <u>College Address</u>
629 Geneva Drive P.O. Box 1430
Tuscaloosa, AL 35160 Stillman College
(205) 362-0206 Tuscaloosa, AL 35403

<u>OBJECTIVE</u>: Staff accountant position with a public accounting firm or a challenging position in a major financial institution where my qualifications will contribute to the profit margin of the company.

EDUCATION: B.S. Business Administration, Stillman College, expected date of Graduation, May 2007. GPA: Overall 3.2 of 4.0, Major 3.5 of 4.0

<u>EXPERIENCE</u>: Fall 1989 Stillman College, Business Department, Tuscaloosa, AL <u>Student Assistant:</u> performed general office work, graded exams. And typed various letter, etc. on the IBM computers and graded papers.

Spring 1990 Stillman College, Business and Finance Lab, Tuscaloosa, AL <u>Tutor:</u> Tutored economics accounting and finance. Also worked on IBM computers and graded papers.

Summer 1989 Sears Accounting Office, Anniston, AL

Assistant Unit Clerk: performed various clerical duties, including taking inventory, and processing records on various computers.

Spring 1989 Stillman College Tax preparer: Volunteer Income Tax Program (VITA). Assisted Elderly and low income individuals in preparing their taxes.

OTHER ACTIVITIES: Alpha Delta Zeta (President), National Honor Society, Business/Economics Club, Students in Free Enterprise (SIFE), Volunteer Income Tax Assistance (VITA), Kennon Investment Group

HONORS: Academic Dean's Scholarship I, AICPA Scholarship, National Dean's List, Mr. Junior UNCF, Who's Who Among American Students

TECHNICAL SKILLS: D-Base IV, IBM, APPLE, VAX, Commodore, Datacard

Cover Letter Format (sample)
Your Present Address
City, State Zip Code
Date
Inside Address
-Name

-Title

-Company Name

-Company Address

Dear (Mr., Ms.)_____:

1st PARAGRAPH, Tell why you are writing, the position or title (if known) and/or the Particular field for which you are applying.

2nd PARAGRAPH Briefly summarize your reasons for desiring this type of position. If you have had experience, be sure to point out particular Achievements or other qualification in this field of work.

Mention some facet of the position which genuinely interests you (this gives the letter a personal touch

Give any additional specialized training/experiences you have had. And relate it to the position.

3rd PARAGRAPH Refer to your enclosed resume (and any additional information) which gives a summary of your qualifications; e.g. education, Career objective, and work experience.

4th PARAGRAPH Have an appropriate closing to pave the way for the interview by asking for an application blank, by giving your phone number, or by offering some similar suggestion for an immediate and Favorable reply.

Sincerely,

(Signed Signature)

(Typed Name)

Once a letter of application has been sent and you do not hear from the prospective employer, or if you receive a letter indicating that the firm is glad to have the resume and is filing it in case an opening occurs, there is no reason to stop expressing interest in the position. Never send off an application without a cover letter.

If you are especially interested in working for a certain employer, do not hesitate to send another letter within two, three, or six months after the first letter. It need not be another complete application; it is just a reminder that you are still interested in being employed by that firm or that you want to provide additional information which may be of importance to the employer.

Sample Cover Letter

3601 Stillman Blvd.

P.O. Box 1430

Tuscaloosa, AL 35403

Oct. 4, 2012

Mr. John Doe
Manager, Professional Employment
XYZ Company
100 S.W. First Street
Anytown, Alabama 00000

Dear Mr. Doe:

I am writing this letter because I am a senior at Stillman College majoring in Business Administration with a concentration in Accounting and seeking a job as a Staff Accountant in your business organization.

My primary goal upon graduating from college is to find a job where my expertise in the accounting field with emphasis in cost accounting and auditing can be fully utilized. Working for XYZ Company would help me achieve this goal. I am convinced that my experience and academic qualifications in dealing with various facets of accounting from medium to large business organization will contribute to your company's goal of providing more competitive services to the general public. I have broadened my intellectual curiosity by taking courses in philosophy, logic, art, music, technical writing, calculus, and econometrics.

The resume that I have enclosed with this letter will give you some background information about me, my education and experiences.

I will appreciate reading or receiving a phone call from you if you consider my credentials worthy of further consideration through an interviewing opportunity. My phone number, email or snail mail addresses are enclosed for your convenience.

Sincerely,

Jane A. Jones
Phone:(205)366-8900
jjones@att.net

Chapter 8

THE INTERVIEW SESSION(S)

What is an interview?

Typically an interview is used as a screening process in which you are given the opportunity to learn more about an organization. At the same time, it is company's opportunity to evaluate you as a prospective employee.

The effective interview is the most important aspect of the employment search. In a 20- or 30-minute interview, your personality, educational background and work experience are appraised. It is usually the most decisive part of your campaign for the job opportunity you want. Initial contacts by letter, resume or application describe one's credentials. The interview demonstrates

Qualities the interviewer looks for: Personality. Be genuine, self-confident, pleasant, and honest. Be your good self.

Articulation. Express yourself clearly and concisely. Answer questions thoroughly and Candidly

Alertness. Make your answers and questions relevant and intelligent. Develop your Questions prior to the interview.

Enthusiasm. Be moderately enthusiastic, optimistic, show an appropriate amount of interest.

Maturity. Express clear professional goal(s). Know what you want.

Conduct yourself as if you are determined to get the job you are discussing in a responsible manner.

Motivation. Show you incentive and willingness through your desire and interest in the Job opportunity. You are your best cheer leader (motivator).

Compatibility. Express, through your behavior, your ability to get along with others and handle any responsibility assigned to you or to your group.

Competition: Show the competitive edge you have over other competitors such as clear understanding of SWOT analysis and Feasibility Study of any business organization as to determine its strengths, weaknesses, opportunities, and threats and recommendations for achieving organizational goal(s).

Preparation. Know relevant information about the company-location, product, and General knowledge about its business purpose. The more you know the Greater impression you will make on the interviewer. Always practice Before an interview. Do some role playing.

POSITIVE INTERVIEW TIPS

Some interviewers like to do most of the talking and judge you by your reactions–the comprehension and intelligence you show. Other interviewers say very little. Their attitude is that it is up to you to sell yourself.

- Approach the interview with a positive attitude and sincere interest in the company.
- Pay attention to your appearance. You want to appear professional, so dress conservatively (dark suit, light shirt)
- No loud ties (male), short dresses or high splits (female)
- Arrive a few minutes early for the conversation
- Be friendly, relaxed; be yourself.
- Maintain good eye contact.
- Communicate accomplishments.

- Do not monopolize the conversation, but be an active participant.
- Be an attentive listener when the interviewer is speaking
- Respond to questions with more than a yes or no answer. Avoid long pauses.
- Show interest through asking well-through-out questions. Ask some definite questions about the company.
- Do not try to fill in the silent spots. You may tend to ramble.
- Display your personality and achievements, initiating as well as responding.
- Accentuate the positive. Be optimistic. Display self-confidence, ambition, competitive attitude. Be sure you good points get across to the interviewer.
- Emphasize your special skills and interests.
- Do not out-price yourself (if possible indicate your salary is negotiable or give a range)

TOUGH INTERVIEW QUESTIONS

1. Why don't you tell me something good about yourself?
2. Why did you last job end?
3. Do you know anything about our company?

"My short-term goal is to bluff my way through this job interview. My long-term goal is to invent a time machine so I can come back and change everything I've said so far."

4. Why do you think you would like doing this job in our company?
5. What qualifications do you have that makes you feel that you would be successful in this position?
6. What do you hope to be doing five or ten year from now?
7. How do you fit in with groups of people who have backgrounds and interests different from you own?
8. Can you take instructions/criticism with getting upset?
9. Do you prefer working with others or by yourself?
10. What would you say is your weakest point?
11. Would you be willing to work overtime.
12. How do you feel about male/female supervisors?
13. What have you done that shows initiative and willingness to work?
14. Will your former employers give you a good reference?
15. Can you tell me why you've been unemployed so long?

16. I see you have children?
17. What would you expect as a starting salary?
18. I've interviewed several people with more experience than you. Why should I hire you instead of them?
19. Do you have any questions?
20. What are your salary expectations?

QUESTIONS YOU MAY ASK DURING INTERVIEWING SESSIONS

- What are the opportunities for advancement?
- Does your company have a practice of promoting on merit and/or promoting from within?
- Describe initial assignments and where I might be assigned. It shows that you are eager to start as soon as possible.
- What opportunities will I have for professional development?
- Does your company encourage and support "continuing education" for its employees?
- Does the company provide tuition reimbursement?
- Tell me about the community in which I would be employed.

Chapter 9

TWENTY-FIVE REASONS WHY APPLICANTS DON'T GET THE JOB

1. Poor appearance.
2. Passive and indifferent attitude.
3. No knowledge of the position or the company.
4. Lack of tact, bad manners.
5. No definite career plans.
6. Insincerity during the interview, shopping around for the best offer.

7. Lack of eye contact and lack of serious preparations.
8. Evasive answers to questions asked.
9. Late for interview
10. Limp handshake.
11. Sloppy resume and application.
12. Poor diction and grammar.
13. Over aggressiveness, conceited manner.
14. Failure to ask questions about the job or the company.
15. Lack of confidence, poise.
16. Overemphasis on money.
17. Condemnation of past employers.
18. Unwilling to relocate.
19. Reluctance to take open position
20. Wanting short-term position.
21. Failure to participate in community activities (not all jobs)
22. Cynical attitude, showing intolerance or prejudice.
23. Demonstrating narrow interests.
24. Not able to take criticisms.
25. Using high pressure tactics.

KEEPING THE JOB

Now that you have found the job, how do you keep it? Beginning a new job is a challenge. It is up to you to rise to the occasion.

Regardless of you credentials, experience, etc., everyone is expendable, and if you do not do a good job, you will need a new job. How do you keep the job?

1. Remember once you are hired, you are on probation and need to prove yourself during the first few months, years, etc.
2. Listen and learn-be receptive, get to know the people you work with.
3. Interact with your co-workers, but do not be misled by what others say; size up situations for yourself and do not get overly involved with office politics.
4. Maintain a professional attitude at all times-make sure you have the edge on your co-workers:- get to work

early—before others, and leave work later. Just because others may come to work a little late and leave a little early does not mean you have to. — be yourself-work twice as hard as your co-workers; prove yourself worthy of the position you have.

5. Be nice to everyone whether they are nice to you or not.
6. Follow procedures—every organization has rules and procedures, follow them.
7. Concentrate on being productive and meeting deadlines. If your boss wants something done by a certain time, work all night, if necessary, to get it done on time.
8. Keep your boss informed of your progress on projects.
9. Have a positive attitude—if you don't like your job, then you do not need to be working there. If you like your job and want to keep it, have a positive attitude and work harder than anyone else

STUDENTS – WHAT DO EMPLOYERS EXPECT OF YOU?
FYI – Come to Work Every Day and On Time
- **Make Smart Decisions at Work and in your personal Life**
- **Follow Directions from your Supervisors Carefully**
- **Concentrate on your Work and Care about the Quality of your Work**
- **Read, Write, and Calculate Very Well**
- **Recognize Problems and Find Solutions**

- Finish a Job When you are Supposed to Without Sacrificing quality
- Be Honest and Dependable
- Work Hard and Take the Lead
- Communicate Very Well and Get Along With Others Especially Customers and Supervisors
- Dress Properly and Practice Good Grooming
- Be Cooperative and Have a Positive Attitude
  Be Drug Free
- Pray To God Every Day For Strength, Energy, Patience, and Good Health

SUCCESS STORIES:

Chichi Chijioke, MD

C*hiChi Chijioke M.D*, Born in Tuscaloosa, AL as well as attended Elementary and High School in Tuscaloosa, AL. Dr. ChiChi Chijioke secured her first degree from Georgetown University, Washington, D.C in Biology and Pre-med. She continued her academic program at the University of Virginia in Charlottesville, VA, with specialization in Emergency Medicine.

During her residency at UNC, she participated in medicine without the bells and whistles in Panama. Dr. ChiChi Chijioke, now happily married, is currently practicing medicine with Pegasus Emergency Group in Birmingham, AL.

Michael Chijioke, JD, MPH. Michael Chijioke was born in Tuscaloosa, AL, attended Elementary and High School in Tuscaloosa, AL. He secured his first degree in Biology at Virginia Tech University. Michael secured his law degree at Howard University and his masters of Public Health from Eastern Virginia Medical School. He did his Practicum Project at Consortium for Infant and Child Health in Norfolk, Virginia. Michael also did his second International Practicum in Public Health and Clinical Projects with Ambassador's Medical in Pucallpa, Peru. He is currently a Contract and Quality Improvement Specialist at Community Care Network of Virginia.

CONCLUSION: YOUR FUTURE

Your teachers and professors from kindergarten to elementary school to high school and to the College or University can only lay the foundation for your future successes to which you have to play your part by working hard with them, your parents, and counselors. Your success will begin by clear planning and SWOT Analysis (Strengths, Weaknesses, Opportunities, and Threats) of your life. If you plan and implement effectively with the guidance in this book "Students' Successful Survival Handbook, your future success will be very bright.

– Emmanuel Chijioke, Ph.D, JD

www.ingramcontent.com/pod-product-compliance
Ingram Content Group UK Ltd.
Pitfield, Milton Keynes, MK11 3LW, UK
UKHW022223230426
12048UKWH00016BA/1017